Countries Around the World

South Korea

Elizabeth Raum

Heinemann Library
Chicago, Illinois

www.capstonepub.com
Visit our website to find out more information about Heinemann-Raintree books.

To order:
☎ Phone 888-454-2279
💻 Visit www.capstonepub.com
to browse our catalog and order online.

©2012 Heinemann Library
an imprint of Capstone Global Library, LLC
Chicago, Illinois

Edited by Abby Colich and Claire Throp
Designed by Ryan Frieson and Steven Mead
Original illustrations © Capstone Global Library, Ltd., 2012
Illustrated by Oxford Designers & Illustrators
Picture research by Ruth Blair
Originated by Capstone Global Library, Ltd.
Printed in China by China Translation and Printing Services

15 14 13 12 11
10 9 8 7 6 5 4 3 2 1

Library of Congress Cataloging-in-Publication Data
Raum, Elizabeth.
  South Korea / Elizabeth Raum.
    p. cm.—(Countries around the world)
  Includes bibliographical references and index.
  ISBN 978-1-4329-6113-8 (hb)—ISBN 978-1-4329-6139-8 (pb)
1. Korea (South)—Juvenile literature. I. Title.
DS902.R36 2012
951.95—dc22   2011015441

Acknowledgments

The author and publishers are grateful to the following for permission to reproduce copyright material: Corbis pp. 8 (© Kim Kyung-hoon/Reuters), 9 (© Bettmann), 10 (© Nathan Benn), 12 (© YNA/epa), 14 (© Philippe Lissac/GODONG), 18 (© Rungroj Yongrit/epa), 20 (© Hussein Malla/POOL/epa), 21 (© Jo Yong-hak/Reuters), 22 (© YONHAP/epa), 26 (© Atlantide Phototravel), 29 (© he lulu/Xinhua Press), 30 (© Michel Setboun); Getty Images pp. 11 (Kim Ho-Young/Korea Pool), 28 (Stephen Lovekin), 33 (Dennis Gottlieb/FoodPix), 35 (Park Yeong-cheol/AFP); iStockphoto p. 25 (© leesungjae); Photolibrary pp. 6 (Fotosearch), 17 (Eric Baccega/Age footstock); Shutterstock pp. 5 (© Steve Rosset), 31 (© Olga Besnard), 38 (© Chen Wei Seng), 46 (© wavebreakmedia ltd).

Cover photograph of the Myeongdong shopping district in Seoul, South Korea reproduced with permission of Corbis (© Lo Mak/Redlink)

We would like to thank Jennifer Jung-Kim for her invaluable help in the preparation of this book.

Every effort has been made to contact copyright holders of any material reproduced in this book. Any omissions will be rectified in subsequent printings if notice is given to the publisher.

Note on Romanization of Korean
McCune-Reischauer is the Romanization method preferred by academics. This is a phonetic system that reflects Korean pronunciation. But some people find this system difficult because it takes time to learn.

Since 2000, the South Korean government has been using a different system that is easier to learn. North Korea uses yet another method of Romanization that also has numerous exceptions, but it is not used in this book except where the name or term is commonly known in the West (for example, Kim Il Sung, Kim Jong Il, Juche).

This book primarily uses the South Korean system except when names are more commonly spelled in a different way (for example, Syngman Rhee and Kim Il Sung). The McCune-Reischauer system is given in parentheses after the first use of the South Korean system.

Contents

Some words in the book are in bold, **like this**. You can find out what they mean by looking in the glossary.

Introducing South Korea

South Korea is a land of contrasts. Modern South Korean companies make cars, ships, computers, and wireless communication systems. Millions of people live in high-rise buildings in clean, modern cities. Seoul, South Korea's capital, is a safe and attractive place for people to live. In 2010, it was named the World Design Capital.

Visitors can see modern buildings and ancient temples on the same tour. South Koreans preserve ancient **shrines** and temples. These very old buildings provide a look into Korea's past life and **culture**. Many South Koreans wear traditional clothing for special occasions. They also hold ceremonies to honor their **ancestors**. South Koreans respect their past, while working to create an even better future.

Where is South Korea?

South Korea is officially called the **Republic** of Korea. It occupies the southern half of the Korean **Peninsula**. It is located between the Yellow Sea and the East Sea. The East Sea extends along the southern coast of South Korea. An **artificial** boundary called the **Demilitarized Zone (DMZ)** separates South Korea from its neighboring country, North Korea. South Korea has a total area of 38,502 square miles (99,720 square kilometers). That is slightly larger than the state of Indiana.

Daily Life

Koreans greet one another with a quick, short bow. The bow is often a nodding of the head. Young people bow to their parents, teachers, and employers. Bowing is a sign of respect.

This is one of the traditional temples that can be found in Seoul.

History: A Land Divided

Stone Age people lived on the Korean **Peninsula** about 40,000 years ago. Today's Koreans trace their **ancestors** to people who arrived from Manchuria, Mongolia, and southern Siberia between 8,000 and 3,000 BCE. These people built villages, raised animals, and wove cloth. They made useful tools and weapons. They also built the first **dolmens**, which are burial tombs. Korea has more dolmens—30,000—than any other place in the world.

Korean kingdoms

Koreans believe their nation began in 2333 BCE, when a leader named Dangun (also called Tan'gun) founded the Old Joseon (also called Choson) Kingdom. Old Joseon lasted for over 2,000 years. For the next several thousand years, various kingdoms ruled Korea. Each one introduced new ideas and customs.

In the year 2000, several dolmen sites in South Korea were set aside as national parks and named UNESCO World Heritage Sites.

In 108 BCE, China's Han **Dynasty** (206 BCE–220 CE) conquered Old Joseon. The Han brought Chinese **culture** and customs to Korea. From 668 to 935 CE, the entire Korean Peninsula came together under the rule of the later Silla Dynasty. Many people in the kingdom became **Buddhist**. Over 200 Buddhist temples were built during this time. Later, Silla grew weak over time, and the Goryeo (also called Koryo) Dynasty (918–1392) gained control. The English word *Korea* comes from the native Korean word *Goryeo*.

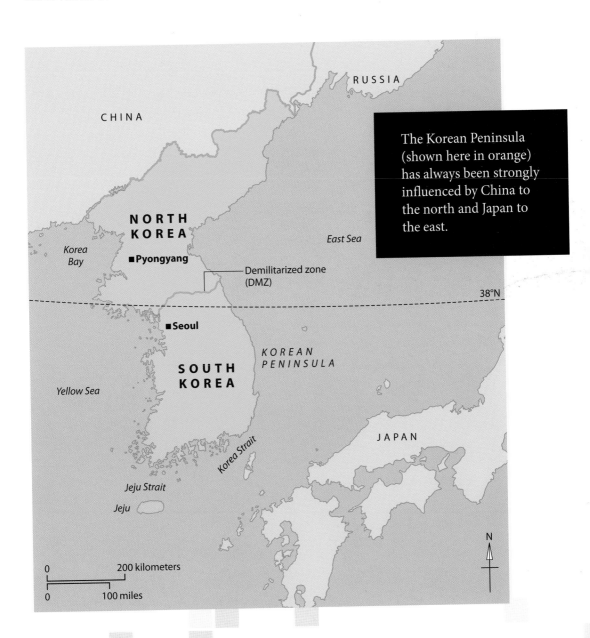

The Korean Peninsula (shown here in orange) has always been strongly influenced by China to the north and Japan to the east.

The Joseon Dynasty

In 1392 the Joseon Dynasty extended Korea's borders north. Hanyang (present-day Seoul) became the capital. Joseon leaders valued education and art. In 1377 they printed the first book in the world using movable type. After repeated attacks and a war with Japan (1592–1598), Joseon rulers closed Korea's borders to outsiders. Korea became known as the Hermit Kingdom. (A hermit is a person who does not interact with the rest of the world.)

YI SUN-SIN (1545-1598)

Yi Sun-sin, one of Korea's greatest heroes, was a naval commander who built the world's first "ironclad" ships, which were ships covered in protective metal. Spikes covered these "turtle ships." A dragon's head held a cannon in its mouth. Yi Sun-sin's forces defeated Japan in the 1500s.

Students study this model of a turtle ship from the 1500s.

In September 1945, U.S. troops marched into southern Korea.

A nation divided

In 1910 Japan made Korea a **colony**. Japan remained in control of Korea until 1945, when World War II ended. Koreans celebrated Japan's defeat. Many Koreans had suffered under Japanese rule. Now they wanted to become independent.

Korea's neighbor, the **Soviet Union**, had worked to defeat Japan. The United States had worked with the Soviet Union. However, the Soviet Union was a **communist** country. The United States did not want Korea to become communist, too. So on August 10 through 11, 1945, U.S. officials split Korea in half along the 38th **parallel**. Troops from the Soviet Union moved into northern Korea. U.S. troops moved into southern Korea.

The Korean War (1950–1953)

On August 15, 1948, South Korea became a **democracy**. Syngman Rhee, the first president, was a Korean educated in the United States. Meanwhile, neighboring North Korea became communist. Both countries began plotting a takeover of each other. North Korea moved first.

On June 25, 1950, North Korean troops crossed the 38th parallel. They overpowered the poorly trained South Korean army and conquered Seoul. The **United Nations (UN)** sent troops from 16 countries to support South Korea. China and the Soviet Union supported North Korea. Almost 3 million people died before fighting ended on July 27, 1953. North Korea and the United States agreed to stop the fighting and create a **Demilitarized Zone (DMZ)** along the 38th parallel, to keep fighting forces separate. The DMZ also forms the border between the two Koreas.

These soldiers are guarding the Demilitarized Zone (DMZ) between South and North Korea. It is about 2.5 miles (4 kilometers) wide.

This family was separated after Korea was divided into two separate countries. They met again in 2010, after 60 years.

South Korea's first presidents were **dictators**. They took away many freedoms from their people. When students and workers revolted, they were punished. Gradually, the government changed. Today, South Korea is a strong democracy. It also has a growing **economy**.

Challenge

Peace with the North is South Korea's biggest challenge today. Despite attempts to make peace, the situation remains tense. For example, in March 2010 a South Korean warship sunk, killing 46 South Korean sailors. South Korea blamed North Korea. In November 2010, North Korean troops fired on a South Korean island, killing two marines and two **civilians**. Threats continue. South Korean leaders seek a solution.

Regions and Resources: Using Land Wisely

Mountains and rolling hills cover about 70 percent of South Korea. The Taebaek (also called T'aebaek) Mountain Range is the largest of five ranges. There are four major rivers—the Nakdong, Han, Geum, and Seomjin—and many smaller ones. Many rivers are dry until spring rains fill them. The only natural lake in South Korea is a crater lake at the top of Mount Halla, the highest mountain, located on Jeju (also called Cheju) Island. South Korea has good harbors and popular beaches. There are 3,000 islands, most with no people living on them. However, the largest island, Jeju, has 500,000 people.

Daily Life

Until the 1980s, few South Koreans owned cars. Once they began buying cars, they could drive to South Korea's beautiful beaches. Many beaches have become family resorts. Koreans enjoy swimming, waterskiing, and windsurfing. Snorkeling, surfing, and **parasailing** are also popular.

Beautiful rolling hills cover much of South Korea.

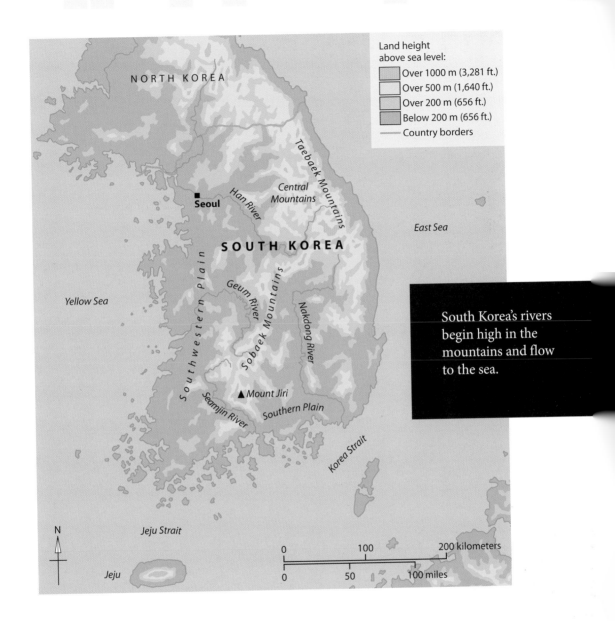

Land height
above sea level:

- Over 1000 m (3,281 ft.)
- Over 500 m (1,640 ft.)
- Over 200 m (656 ft.)
- Below 200 m (656 ft.)
- Country borders

NORTH KOREA

Taebaek Mountains

Central Mountains

Han River

Seoul

East Sea

SOUTH KOREA

Geum River

Yellow Sea

Southwestern Plain

Sobaek Mountains

Nakdong River

South Korea's rivers begin high in the mountains and flow to the sea.

▲ Mount Jiri

Seamjin River

Southern Plain

Korea Strait

N

Jeju Strait

0   100   200 kilometers

0   50   100 miles

Jeju

Climate

Korea has four distinct seasons. It is similar to many Mid-Atlantic U.S. states, such as New York and Pennsylvania. August is the hottest month. Summers are rainy, with temperatures that average 79°F (26°C). Winters are cold, with temperatures just below freezing. It is warmer near the coasts and cooler farther north.

Farming

Most Korean farms are small. However, as young people move to the cities, large company-run farms are becoming more common. Korean farms grow rice, barley, wheat, and a variety of vegetables. Fruit, cotton, tobacco, and **ginseng**, an herb used in medicines, grow well in Korea. Some farmers raise cattle and chickens. South Korea has to **import** food to meet all its needs.

Rice, South Korea's most important crop, is grown in wet paddy fields like these near Seoul.

Fishing

Fishing is one of Korea's major **industries**. Anchovy, squid, and mackerel make up half the catch. Yellow croaker and swordfish are important, too. From 1987 to 2000, Korean fishermen **exported** fish to other nations. Beginning in 2001, however, the growing population had to import fish to meet its needs at home.

Industry

About 20 percent of South Koreans work in **manufacturing** and industry. Coal mining was important before 1990. But as people switched to using oil and new kinds of energy, mining declined. Mines now produce limestone and small amounts of gold, silver, and other minerals.

Korea has many small manufacturing firms producing chemicals, paints, and farm equipment. There are also large family-run businesses, called *jaebeol* (also called *chaebol*). Samsung (electronics), Hyundai (automobiles), and LG (electronics and chemicals) are examples of *jaebeol*. Korea is one of the largest producers of computer chips and of ships.

Wildlife: Land of the Moon Bear

Korea was once home to Siberian tigers, leopards, bears, wolves, and foxes. Today, these animals are rare. Deer, wild boars, raccoon dogs, rabbits, and badgers still live in the mountains. Korea has about 50 **species** of native birds. About 380 species migrate, or travel, through Korea in the spring and fall.

YOUNG PEOPLE

Seoul's Children's Grand Park is specially designed for children. There is a zoo, which has tigers, elephants, jaguars, meerkats, and penguins. In all, there are 623 animals from 106 different species. The park also includes gardens, a water play area, and amusement rides.

Map legend:
- Mountainous National Parks
- Marine and Coastal National Parks
- Historical National Parks

NORTH KOREA

Seoul

SOUTH KOREA

▲ Mount Jiri

N

0   100   200 kilometers
0   50   100 miles

South Korea has fifteen mountain national parks, four marine and coastal national parks, and one historical park.

Environmentalists are trying to save **endangered** species such as the leopard cat, the Russian rat snake, and the Asiatic black bear (moon bear). Environmentalists had thought moon bears died out—until they discovered six of them in Mt. Jiri (Mt. Chiri) National Park in 2001. They hope to increase the population to 50 by 2012. In the past, moon bears were killed for their meat or used in traditional Chinese medicines.

Plants and flowers

Over 4,500 plant species grow on the Korean **Peninsula**, including the rose, iris, and daisy. **Ginseng** grows wild. The mountains are covered with pine and spruce trees. Maple, oak, elm, and other leaf-bearing trees turn beautiful colors every fall.

Daily Life

Koreans enjoy hiking in the mountains. National parks include hiking trails. Some are so long that it takes three days to complete the hike. There are campsites and shelters along the way.

Korean moon bears eat fruits and vegetables, honey, and insects.

Infrastructure: Looking to the Future

South Korea is a **democracy**. Presidents are elected for a single five-year term. The president appoints a prime minister and other officials. South Korea's first **constitution**, adopted on July 17, 1948, has been rewritten several times. It grants freedom of religion, the right to own property, and the right to vote.

LEE MYUNG-BAK
(BORN 1941)

Lee Myung-bak came from a poor family. He worked his way through college. In 1965 he began working for Hyundai Engineering as a manager. He worked his way up to head the company. In 2002 he became mayor of Seoul. He was elected president of South Korea in 2007.

South Korea's population, life expectancy, population growth, and **median** age have undergone major changes since 1960. Today fewer babies are being born, people are living longer, and the population is growing older.

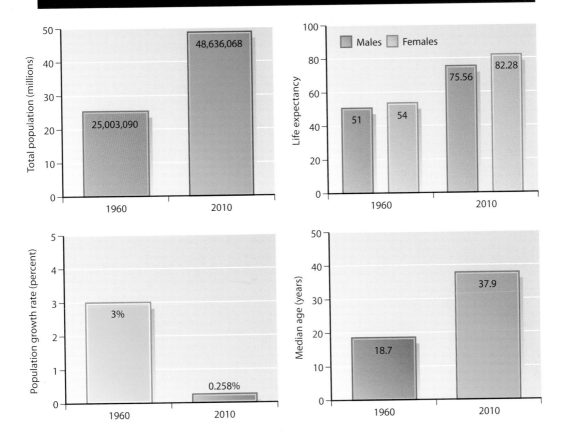

One Korea

The South Korean government has a long-term goal of becoming **unified** with North Korea. Recent South Korean presidents have tried to work with North Korea. In 1998 President Kim Dae-jung introduced the Sunshine Policy, in hopes of establishing peace. Recently, however, North Korea's threats against the South have made it unlikely the two countries will be unified in the near future.

Health care

The Ministry of Health and Social Affairs is a government department that supports health programs throughout South Korea. Almost everyone has medical insurance. Good medical care helps people live longer. At the same time, people are having fewer children. This means that the population is aging faster than anywhere else in the world. An aging population means fewer workers. It can also mean higher health care costs. Older people need more care and require more medicines.

Transportation and communication

South Korea has excellent transportation and communication systems. Products are shipped all over the world by air and boat. Until recently, car ownership in South Korea was lower than in other Asian nations, but this is changing. Even so, many people use public transportation. Subways and taxis are available almost everywhere.

BAN KI-MOON (BORN 1944)

Since 2007 the secretary-general of the **United Nations (UN)**, Ban Ki-moon, has helped to settle conflicts between nations. Before becoming secretary-general, Ban was in charge of South Korea's Ministry of Foreign Affairs and Trade. He speaks Korean, English, and French.

South Korea's Ban Ki-moon is secretary-general of the UN.

YOUNG PEOPLE

All healthy young men are required to serve in the military for about two years after they finish school. Military service is not required of women. In 2010 about 687,000 soldiers were serving in South Korea's army, navy, and air force.

South Korea has seven radio networks, including **Buddhist**, Christian, and public stations. Over 200 television stations provide news, educational programs, and entertainment programs. Many people rely on the Internet and cell phones. By 2010 South Korea had more cell phones than people.

Women's roles

Women have the same rights as men in South Korea. Since 2004, 50 percent of the candidates running for the National Assembly must be women. In 2001 a government department called the Ministry of Gender Equality and Family was established to promote women's rights. Even so, women make only about half as much money as men. Today, many women still face old-fashioned ideas at work or when they run for political office.

These students in Daegu
use laptop computers
instead of textbooks.

Education

South Koreans value education. The **literacy rate** is 97.9 percent. This means that almost everyone over the age of 15 can read and write. For Korean parents and grandparents, education was the key to a successful future. Today, they push their children to do well in school, too.

Elementary school is free. Children begin school at age six. Elementary school lasts six years, middle school lasts three, and high school is another three. In elementary school, students study the Korean language, social studies, mathematics, science, physical education, and fine arts such as music and dance. In third grade, students begin learning English.

Daily Life

South Korean students attend school Monday through Friday and some Saturday mornings. A school day lasts eight hours, and a school year lasts 220 days. That is about 40 days more than most U.S. school years. Many South Korean students also go to private tutors until 10:00 at night to study for college entrance exams.

Students must pay to attend middle and high school. Many parents choose private schools to give their children a better chance of getting into college. Less than half of Korean students attend college. There are 435 colleges and universities in South Korea.

YOUNG PEOPLE

Many Korean parents send their children to schools in the United States and the United Kingdom. In 2008, 27,350 students in grades Kindergarten to 12 studied in different countries. College students study abroad, too. In 2009, 113,519 South Korean students attended colleges overseas. Only China sends more university students overseas.

Culture: Meeting of Old and New

South Korea's **constitution** grants freedom of religion. Roughly half of South Koreans practice some form of religion. Most believers are Christian (29.2 percent) or **Buddhist** (22.8 percent). Some people follow **Islam** or **Judaism**. Many other religious movements exist in this **tolerant** country.

Shamanism, an ancient Korean religion, is still practiced by many. Shamanists believe that spirits filled the world. Special people called shamans are thought to communicate with helpful or harmful spirits by chanting and performing special dances.

Confucianism

Confucianism is not a religion. It is a way of thinking that has influenced Korean life for more than 1,000 years. Confucius (551–479 BCE) was a Chinese philosopher who developed this belief system to create harmony, or agreement, among people. He taught that people are not equal. For example, parents teach and protect children, while children obey and respect parents. Relationships are about responsibility and respect. Honoring the memory of important **ancestors** is an important part of Confucianism.

Daily Life

Korean is spoken by people in both South Korea and North Korea. The grammar of Korean is similar to Japanese, but about 70 percent of Korean words come from Chinese.

YOUNG PEOPLE

In South Korea, when a baby is born, he or she is said to be in a first year. But in a new calendar year, a baby is said to enter a second year. For example, a baby born on December 15 is in her first year, but two weeks later, on January 1, she is said to enter her second year. If asked, her parents would say she is two years old, because she has lived during two different years. This means a child considered to be a 10-year-old in Korea is at least one year younger than a 10-year-old in the United States.

Koreans dress in colorful traditional clothing on New Year's Day and for other special occasions.

Traditional Korean homes are built in an L-shape. Rooms are placed side-by-side along the inside wall, and they open on to a fenced courtyard. The backs of the room form the outside wall of the house. Anyone passing by cannot see into the courtyard. The living space is private. The kitchen is built lower than the other rooms. To provide heat, pipes run from the cooking stove beneath the floor of the house. This system is called *ondol*. It is so popular that even modern city apartments have heating pipes beneath the floors.

These village homes mainly have tile roofs but some have thatched roofs.

Homes

Until the late 1900s, most Koreans lived in farm villages. Children, parents, and grandparents lived together in one home. Today, 81 percent of the people live in big cities. City dwellers often live in apartments in high-rise buildings. These apartments are often very small, so grandparents live separately.

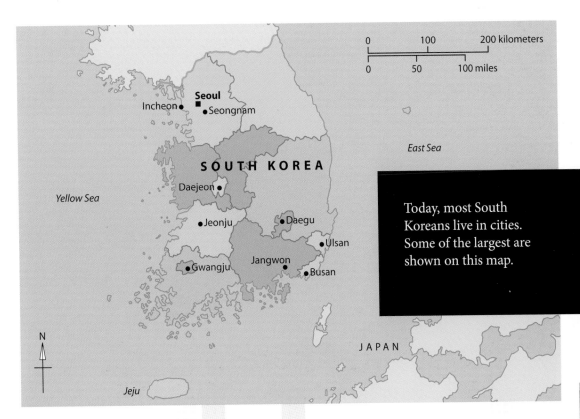

Today, most South Koreans live in cities. Some of the largest are shown on this map.

Music and art

Koreans have a long musical tradition. Ancient music and Korean folk tunes are performed at special concerts. These concerts include some of the 60 musical instruments of ancient Korea. Today, however, most people listen to pop music. South Korean radio stations play jazz, hip-hop, and rap—whatever young people want to hear.

YOUNG PEOPLE

The most popular music today among young South Koreans is K-pop, a kind of pop music often featuring "girl groups." These groups combine simple tunes with rap, an electronic beat, and easy-to-learn dance steps. Groups like Wonder Girls, 2NE1, KARA, After School, and 4Minutes have fans of all ages throughout Asia. Their worldwide audience is growing. Wonder Girls sing their hit "Nobody" in both Korean and English. In 2009 they toured with the Jonas Brothers.

The Wonder Girls, shown here, are one of South Korea's most popular groups.

Ancient art—furniture, metalwork, and pottery—are highly prized today. Art museums throughout the world display Korean art, especially pottery, **calligraphy**, and painting. Modern artists continue to produce works of beauty. Seoul, Busan (also called Pusan), Daegu, and other major cities have art museums open to the public.

This 11-year-old girl practices writing calligraphy.

Daily Life

The Korean alphabet, called *Hangeul*, has 24 symbols. It was invented in 1446 so that Koreans could learn to read. At the time, educated people wrote Chinese, which has about 6,000 characters. Today, about 1,800 Chinese characters are still in use in Korea, but everyone reads and writes using *Hangeul*.

How to say...

| **Hello/goodbye** | *Annyeong haseyo* (Ahn-nyoung ha-say-yo) |
| **Thank you** | *Gamsa hamnida* (Gahm-sa hahm-nida) |

Children who are especially good at soccer attend private soccer schools.

Sports

Tae kwon do, a martial art used for self-defense, began in Korea over 2,000 years ago. It is South Korea's national sport. *Ssireum*, which is Korean wrestling, developed 1,500 years ago. Today, national tournaments are held eight times a year. The champion's title is "Strongest Man Under the Heavens."

Soccer is extremely popular. In 2002 South Korea and Japan hosted the first World Cup held in Asia. They built modern stadiums that are now used by 15 professional teams. Baseball is also popular. Youth soccer and baseball teams compete internationally. South Korean baseball teams play in the Asia-Pacific Region Little League Championships, competing for a chance to play in the Little League World Series held yearly in Williamsport, Pennsylvania.

The Olympics

South Korea first participated in the 1948 Olympics in London, England. Since then South Korean athletes have won 85 gold, 82 silver, and 79 bronze medals. The strongest performances are in speed skating, judo, archery, and wrestling. In 1988 South Korea hosted the Olympics in Seoul. Figure skater Kim Yu-na won gold in the 2010 Olympics held in Vancouver, Canada.

YOUNG PEOPLE

In 2000 the World Cyber Games began in Korea. Nearly one-third of South Koreans play online games called eSports. The most popular is StarCraft, a science fiction game. Major companies such as Samsung and SK Telecom sponsor teams that play in online tournaments. These players, mostly young people, are treated like celebrities. The tournaments are broadcast on television.

Kim Yu-na competed for South Korea in a figure skating competition in Paris in 2009.

Entertainment

People throughout South Korea enjoy movies, television, and sporting events. City dwellers enjoy going to the theater to see plays or operas. Summer sports include hiking, golf, mountain biking, and scuba diving. In winter, people ice skate, ski, and snowboard. There are 14 ski resorts in South Korea, and more are being built.

Foods

Rice is the basis of most Korean meals. *Gimchi* (also called *kimch'i*), a pickled vegetable dish, is made of cabbage with added spices. It is served at most meals, along with rice, soup, and various side dishes. Adding red pepper paste and garlic makes Korean soups and rice hot and spicy. South Koreans eat more garlic per person than people in any other country. The most popular meat dish is *bulgogi* (also called *pulgogi*). It is made of thin strips of lean beef barbecued over hot coals. Fish, pork, and poultry are popular, too.

South Koreans drink tea with their meals. Coffee is also becoming popular. They finish a meal by drinking a broth made from water boiled in the rice pot. They usually eat fruit for dessert.

Daily Life

Koreans do not use forks or knives when eating Korean food. They use spoons for mixing and stirring, and for eating soup and rice. They use chopsticks for meat and side dishes. They rarely eat with their fingers.

Cold cucumber soup

This soup is often eaten on hot summer days. Be sure to have an adult help you when using the stove or pouring the soup into bowls.

Ingredients

3 small cucumbers, cut matchstick thin

1 tsp. crushed chili pepper (*gochu garu*)

$1/4$ cup cider vinegar

1 tbsp. sugar

2 tbsp. soy sauce

1 tbsp. sesame oil

4 cups water

Ice cubes, for serving

2 tsp. sesame seeds (optional)

What to do

1. In a large bowl, mix the matchstick cucumbers with the chili pepper, vinegar, sugar, soy sauce, and sesame oil.

2. Let the cucumbers sit in the seasoning for 10 minutes.

3. Add water.

4. Chill in the refrigerator.

5. Add sesame seeds and ice cubes before serving.

6. Ladle into individual bowls.

South Korea Today

South Korea's greatest challenge today is its relationship with North Korea. Both countries want a **unified** Korea. They share the same history and language. They both value education. However, South Korea is larger, wealthier, and healthier. North Korea has a struggling **economy**, but it has a huge army and **nuclear weapons**. Many South Koreans worry about an attack from the North such as the one that happened in November 2010.

The future

Despite this overwhelming challenge, South Korea is moving boldly into the future. South Korea has good relations with many other countries, a strong economy, and an excellent communication system. Like China, India, and Japan, South Korea has entered the space race. In August 2009 and June 2010, South Korean scientists attempted to launch satellites into space. Both launches failed, but South Korea's space program will continue. South Koreans have always worked hard to reach their goals.

Comparing North and South Korea

	South Korea	North Korea
Population	48,754,657 (2011 est.)	24,457,492 (2011 est.)
Government	Democracy	Communist dictatorship
Per capita income (average money earned in each household)	$28,500 (2009 est.)	$1,800 (2009 est.)
Life expectancy	79.05 years (2011 est.)	68.89 years (2011 est.)
Telephones	19.29 million (2009)	1.18 million (2008)
Nuclear weapons	No	Yes

Since 1948, the two Koreas have made different choices.

Daily Life

South Koreans and North Koreans speak the same language. However, the dialect (local version of the language) spoken in the South is *Hangugeo* (also called *Han'gugo*). In North Korea the dialect is called *Joseonmal* (also called *Chosonmal*). People can usually understand one another, but they spell words differently.

Schoolchildren in Goheung, near the Naro Space Center, cheer for the 2010 rocket launch.

YOUNG PEOPLE

On the first anniversary of a child's birth, families celebrate with a look into the future. The child is given a choice of several items that may predict his or her future. A gold coin means wealth. A pen means life as a writer. A piece of thread means long life. A book means life as a scholar.

Fact File

Official name: **Republic** of Korea

Nationality: Korean

Official language: Korean

Capital city: Seoul

Bordering countries: North Korea to the north

Population: 48,754,657 (July 2011 est.)

Largest cities (populations): Seoul (9,778 million) (2003 figure)
Busan (3,439 million)
Incheon (2,572 million) (part of Seoul metropolitan area)
Daegu (2,369,800)

System of government: Republic

Date of independence: August 15, 1945 (from Japan)

Date of constitution: Current **constitution** approved on October 29, 1987

Religion: Christian (29.2 percent), **Buddhist** (22.8 percent), none (46.5 percent)

Life expectancy: 79.05 years (2011 est.)

Literacy rate: 97.9 percent

Climate: Moderate temperatures, with four seasons

Area (total): 38,502 square miles (99,720 square kilometers)

Coastline: 1,499 miles (2,413 kilometers)

Longest river: Nakdong, 324 miles (521 kilometers)

Highest elevation: Mount Halla, 6,398 feet (1,950 meters)

Lowest elevation: East Sea, 0 feet (0 meters)

Local currency: Won (₩)

Agriculture products: Rice, root crops, barley, vegetables, fruits; cattle, pigs, chickens, milk, eggs; fish

Major industries: Electronics, telecommunications, automobile production, chemicals, shipbuilding, steel

Imports: Machinery, electronics and electronic equipment, oil, steel, transportation equipment, organic chemicals, plastics

Exports: Semiconductors, wireless telecommunications equipment, motor vehicles, computers, steel, ships, chemical products

Major markets: China (21.5 percent), United States (10.9 percent), Japan (6.6 percent), Hong Kong (4.6 percent) (2008)

Major suppliers: China (17.7 percent), Japan (14 percent), United States (8.9 percent), Saudi Arabia (7.8 percent), United Arab Emirates (4.4 percent), Australia (4.1 percent) (2008)

National flower: *Mugunghwa* (Rose of Sharon)

National coat of arms: Adopted in 1963, it features a symbol called *taeguk* bordered by five petals and a ribbon bearing the inscription "The Republic of Korea" in *Hangeul* characters. The *taeguk* can also be seen on the flag on page 46.

Famous South Koreans: Ban Ki-moon (born 1944), secretary-general of the **UN**
Kim Dae-jung (born 1925), president of South Korea, winner of 2000 Nobel Peace Prize for efforts to achieve peace with North Korea
Kim Yu-na (born 1990) 2010 Olympic gold medal ice skater
Moon Dae-sung (born 1976) 2004 Olympic gold medalist in **tae kwon do**
Park Ji-Sung (born 1981) soccer player for the English team Manchester United
Rain (born 1982) pop singer

Children learn tae kwon do, the national sport.

National holidays:

January 1	New Year's Day
Lunar calendar New Year (1st day of 1st month)	Seolla
March 1	Independence Movement Day
May 5	Children's Day
Lunar calendar (8th day of 4th month)	Buddha's Birthday
June 6	Memorial Day
August 15	Liberation Day
Lunar calendar (15th day of 8th month)	Chuseok (Harvest Festival)
October 3	National Foundation Day
December 25	Christmas

National anthem
"Aegukga" ("Love the Country")

Rose of Sharon, thousand miles of range and river land! Guarded by her people, ever may Korea stand!

Until the East Sea's waves are dry, (and) Mt. Baektusan worn away, God watch o'er our land forever! Our Korea manse!

Like that Mt. Namsan armored pine, standing on duty still, wind or frost, unchanging ever, be our resolute will.

In autumn's arching evening sky, crystal, and cloudless blue, Be the radiant moon our spirit, steadfast, single, and true.

With such a will, (and) such a spirit, loyalty, heart and hand, Let us love, come grief, come gladness, this, our beloved land!

Timeline

BCE means Before the Common Era. When this appears after a date, it refers to the number of years before the Christian religion began. BCE dates are always counted backward.

CE means Common Era. When this appears after a date, it refers to the time after the Christian religion began.

BCE

28,000	Ancient people live on the Korean **Peninsula**.
3000	**Ancestors** of modern Korean people move to the Korean Peninsula from Asia.
2333	Dangun founds the Old Joseon Kingdom.
108	China conquers the northern part of Korea.
57	The kingdoms of Goguryeo, Silla, and Baekje are formed.

CE

300s	The Goguryeo Kingdom becomes **Buddhist**.
668	Korea becomes **unified** under the Silla Kingdom.
935	Wang Geon, the founder of the Goryeo **Dynasty**, rules Korea.
1231	Mongols invade Korea.
1392	Yi Seonggye, the founder of the new Joseon Dynasty, becomes ruler.
1446	The Korean alphabet is invented.
1600s	Manchurians invade Korea.
1876	Japan forces Korea to become a trading partner.
1910	Japan claims Korea as a **colony**.

1945	Korea is divided into two separate territories. The United States oversees South Korea, while the **Soviet Union** oversees North Korea.
1950–1953	North Korea invades South Korea. The **UN** sends troops to assist South Korea. A truce (agreement) is declared in 1953.
1988	Seoul hosts the Summer Olympics.
1998	President Kim Dae-jung begins the Sunshine Policy to encourage open relations with North Korea.
2000	President Kim Dae-jung meets with North Korean President Kim Jong Il in Pyongyang, the capital of North Korea. This is the first meeting between the two countries in 55 years.
2000	President Kim Dae-jung becomes the first South Korean to win the Nobel Peace Prize.
2002	South Korea hosts the FIFA (soccer) World Cup.
2007	South Korea's foreign minister, Ban Ki-moon, becomes secretary general of the UN; Korea elects Lee Myung-bak as its tenth president.
2008	President Lee announces a new environmentally friendly policy.
2010	Seoul is named the 2010 World Design Capital, based on its use of architecture to improve city life.

Glossary

ancestor person from whom an individual is descended; someone more distant than a grandparent

artificial human-made; not natural

Buddhist of the religion Buddhism, originated in India by Buddha (Siddhartha Gautama)

calligraphy beautiful penmanship, especially highly decorative handwriting

civilian person who is not a member of the military

colony area ruled by another country

communist person or country that practices a social system in which all people share work and property

constitution system of laws and principles that govern a nation, state, or corporation

culture practices, beliefs, and traditions of a society

Demilitarized Zone (DMZ) artificial boundary between North and South Korea about 2.5 miles (4 kilometers) wide, designed to keep their fighting forces separated

democracy government by the people; a form of government in which power is given to the people and exercised directly by them or by their elected agents, under a free election system

dictator ruler with absolute power over the people

dolmen kind of burial tomb

dynasty series of rulers from the same family or group

economy having to do with the money, industries, and jobs in a country

endangered at risk of being completely killed off

environmentalist someone who works to protect the air, water, animals, plants, and other natural resources from pollution or its effects

export to ship goods to other countries for sale or exchange

ginseng herb used in medicine

import to bring in from a foreign country for use or sale

industry general business activity or trade

Islam religion founded in Saudi Arabia during the 600s CE based on the teachings of Muhammad

Judaism religion that began among ancient Hebrews. They believe in one god.

literacy rate number of adults over the age of 15 who can read and write

manufacturing making or producing a product by hand or machinery

median middle value in a set of data

nuclear weapon missile or bomb that uses energy made by splitting atoms

parallel any of the imaginary lines equidistant from the equator and representing degrees of latitude on Earth's surface

parasailing sport of soaring in a parachute while being pulled along usually by a motorboat

peninsula land area almost completely surrounded by water and connected to the mainland by a narrow strip of land

republic independent country with a head of government who is not a king or queen

shrine sacred or holy place

Soviet Union former union of 15 republics in Eastern Europe and Asia that ended in 1991

species particular type of animal or plant

tae kwon do Korean martial art used in self-defense

tolerant able to accept the beliefs or opinions of others

unify make into a single unit

United Nations (UN) international organization formed in 1945 to promote world peace

Find Out More

Books

Miller, Jennifer A. *South Korea (Country Explorers)*. Minneapolis: Lerner, 2010.

Santella, Andrew. *The Korean War (We the People)*. Minneapolis: Compass Point, 2007.

Walters, Tara. *South Korea (A True Book)*. New York: Children's Press, 2008.

Websites

https://www.cia.gov/library/publications/the-world-factbook/index. html

The World Factbook provides information on the history, people, government, geography, and more of South Korea and over 250 other nations.

http://english.visitkorea.or.kr/enu/index.kto

To plan a trip to Korea—real or imaginary—visit Korea's official tourism website.

www.timeforkids.com/TFK/kids/hh/goplaces/main/0,28375,927166,00. html

Learn more about South Korea at Time for Kids.

http://kids.nationalgeographic.com/kids/places/find/south-korea/

Watch a video about the women divers of South Korea's Jeju Island at this website.

http://english.visitkorea.or.kr/enu/AK/AK_EN_1_4_1.jsp

Learn about South Korea's national symbols at this website.

http://moonbears.org/

Learn more about efforts to protect moon bears.

http://news.bbc.co.uk/2/hi/asia-pacific/country_profiles/1123668.stm

Find out about South Korea on the BBC's website.

www.un.org/sg/
Meet Ban Ki-moon, secretary general of the United Nations, by visiting his web page.

www. indiana.edu/~koreanrs/hangul.html
See *Hangeul* symbols and listen to the Korean language at this website.

Places to visit

Visit South Korea. It is a popular place for tourists. Many tour companies offer trips that include visits to historical sites and national parks, as well as to modern cities such as Seoul and Busan.

Children's Grand Park, Seoul
The Children's Grand Park includes a zoo, gardens, a playground, and an amusement park designed especially for children.

Gyeongju historic sites
Learn about the ancient Silla Dynasty in the city of Gyeongju by visiting ancient shrines, temples, and the Gyeongju National Museum. This city is about an hour north of Busan.

Mt. Sorak National Park
This large national park is located on the northeastern coast of South Korea along the East Sea. Hiking trails lead up Mt. Sorak, the second highest mountain on mainland South Korea with an elevation over 5,000 feet (1,524 meters). Hike up to the Bronze Buddha statue or check out the tall waterfalls along the Flying Dragon trail.

Jeju Island
Visit the Jeju Folk Museum or the Seongeup Folk Village on South Korea's largest island. There's also a Teddy Bear Museum and an Elephant Show with elephants playing basketball, football, and bowling.

Topic Tools

You can use these topic tools for your school projects. Trace the flag and map on to a sheet of paper, using the thick black outlines to guide you. Then color in your pictures. Make sure you use the right colors for the flag!

The South Korean flag, called the *taegeukgi*, has three parts. There's a white background. White is the traditional color of the Korean people. In the center is a red and blue yin-yang symbol. It stands for unity. The four black symbols in the corners represent heaven, moon, sun, and earth. The flag was adopted in 1882.

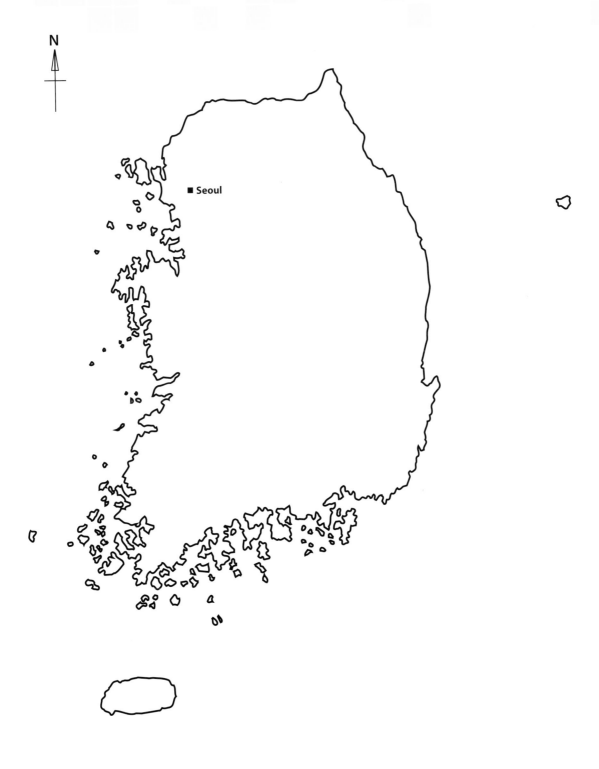

Index